ARMY CHILDHOOD
BRITISH ARMY CHILDREN'S
LIVES AND TIMES

Clare Gibson

Published in Great Britain in 2012 by Shire Publications
Ltd, Midland House, West Way, Botley, Oxford OX2 0PH,
United Kingdom.

44-02 23rd Street, Suite 219, Long Island City, NY 11101,
USA.

E-mail: shire@shirebooks.co.uk   www.shirebooks.co.uk

A CIP catalogue record for this book is available from the
British Library.

Shire Library no. 671.   ISBN-13: 978 0 74781 099 5

Clare Gibson has asserted her right under the Copyright,
Designs and Patents Act, 1988, to be identified as the
author of this book.

Designed by Tony Truscott Designs, Sussex, UK
and typeset in Perpetua and Gill Sans.

Printed in China through Worldprint Ltd.

12 13 14 15 16   10 9 8 7 6 5 4 3 2 1

COVER IMAGE

For caption, see page 8.

TITLE PAGE IMAGE

Pictured in a Royal Munster Fusiliers workshop in India in
around 1910, a pioneer sergeant holds a tool in each hand
as he draws his small son close. Soldiers' sons – themselves
potential future soldiers – were encouraged to learn trades.

CONTENTS PAGE IMAGE

A photograph dating from the second half of the
nineteenth century shows a sergeant and his family outside
their married quarters. The birdcages hanging by the front
door add a homely touch to the wooden walls.

DEDICATION

This book is dedicated to all British army children, past
and present.

ACKNOWLEDGEMENTS

I am grateful to those who gave their permission for their
images to be used in this book and who helped with the
picture research. Thank you, too, to those who have
contributed information, images, and particularly their
stories, to The Army Children Archive (TACA), thereby
helping to build a vivid picture of life as an army child.
And, finally, thanks to my parents, Colonel John Gibson
(Royal Signals) and Marianne Gibson, without whom I
would not have experienced my own army childhood.

Illustrations are acknowledged as follows:

BFBS (British Forces Broadcasting Service), pages 49 and
50; A. W. Cockerill and Peter Goble, pages 36 and 38;
Clare Gibson, pages 13 (top), 42 (top), 51 (bottom) and
54; Maurice Hann, page 43 (top); Maggie Johns (née
Sorrell), pages 17, 41 (top) and 52; A. J Malan, page 34
(bottom); Elizabeth Mardel-Ferreira, page 39 (bottom);
Doreen McKeown (née Routledge), page 15 (bottom);
Judith Millidge, pages 8 (top) and 34 (top); NAAFI (Navy,
Army and Air Force Institutes), page 47; Courtesy of the
Council of the National Army Museum, London, pages 1,
3, 4, 9 (top and bottom) and 18 (top); Barbara Rayner
(née Messenger), page 41 (bottom); Leslie Rutledge, page
26 (bottom); The Army Children Archive (TACA), pages
6, 8 (bottom), 10, 11, 12 (top and bottom), 13 (bottom),
14, 15 (top), 16, 19 (top and bottom), 20, 22, 23 (top and
bottom), 24, 25 (top and bottom), 26 (top), 27, 28, 29,
30 (top and bottom), 32 (top and bottom), 33, 37, 39
(top), 40 (top and bottom), 44, 46 (top, left and right, and
bottom), 48 (top and bottom), 51 (top); The
Wilhelmshaven Association, page 42 (bottom); The
Wyvern Club, page 43 (bottom).

Shire Publications is supporting the Woodland Trust, the UK's leading woodland conservation charity, by funding the dedication of trees.

CONTENTS

THE ARMY CHILD EXPERIENCE

A RMY CHILDREN no longer literally 'follow the drum', as some did, for example, during the Peninsular War, trudging behind columns of soldiers on the march, but typically still spend much of their childhood on the move as they accompany a military parent from posting to posting with their families. Siblings may consequently not only have different birthplaces, then as now, but may even be born in different countries, even though the geographical scope of accompanied postings has shrunk significantly in comparison to previous centuries, reflecting Britain's reduced role on the world stage.

Similarly, although the modes of transport and types of accommodation experienced by army children have changed for the better over time, mirroring advances made by society as a whole, the army generally continues to have a hand in ferrying its soldiers' dependants from posting to posting, and in providing them with accommodation on their arrival. And while some army families perpetuate the long tradition of sending their children to boarding schools in the hope of minimising the disruption to their education caused by frequent moves, others opt for day schools, these being either civilian schools or the service schools whose evolution can be traced back to the regimental schools established during the nineteenth century.

Army children are no different from anyone else in benefiting from the fruits of progress: new technology has made it far easier than in the past to keep in touch with friends and family when posted away, for instance. And being first and foremost children, army children have much in common with their peers of all backgrounds and nationalities. Nevertheless, it is often not appreciated that the sons and daughters of serving soldiers grow up with a foot in both civilian and army camps, nor are the full implications – ranging from the obvious to the subtle – of an upbringing linked to the military way of life fully understood.

An army childhood therefore remains an unconventional childhood, as those who experienced it themselves can testify, particularly with the benefit of hindsight. But what, exactly, makes the army child experience so remarkable? That is what this book seeks to explain.

Opposite:
This nineteenth-century army child was clearly doted upon by his or her father, a corporal in the British Army during Queen Victoria's reign. Having a father in uniform made for an unusual childhood, then as now.

Stuart Lancaster & Son

Chatham Intra
ROCHESTER.

High Street Blue Town
SHEERNESS.

CHILDREN OF THE REGIMENT

S OME MAINTAIN that the British Army was established in 1689, when the standing army that we recognise today was created; others, that it came into being in 1707, with the Act of Union that united England (and Wales) with Scotland. A mere eighteen years separates the two dates on which it is claimed that the status of Britain's professional soldiers – then, but no longer, exclusively men – was regularised, but it makes little difference to the history of army children. For while the foundation of its standing army may have put the position of Britain's soldiers on a more secure footing, it did little for their families. Indeed, it was not until the nineteenth century that the military authorities began officially to assume some sort of responsibility for their soldiers' spouses and children.

Like most large organisations, the British Army is underpinned by a rigid social hierarchy. Its members are categorised by military rank, the expectation being that, after joining up, soldiers will gradually be promoted to higher ranks (although demotion is possible, too). Ranks' names have varied over time, but, broadly speaking, field marshals stand at the apex of the military pyramid, supported, in descending tiers, by generals, lieutenant generals, major generals, brigadiers, colonels, lieutenant colonels, majors, captains, lieutenants and second lieutenants – these make up the commissioned 'officer ranks'. Below the commissioned officers come the 'other ranks', starting with the warrant officers, comprising warrant officers class 1, or WO1s (also known as regimental sergeant majors), and warrant officers class 2, or WO2s (these being company or squadron sergeant majors). And, finally, the bottom section of the military pyramid consists of non-commissioned officers, or NCOs, senior NCOs being staff or colour sergeants and sergeants, and junior NCOs being corporals and lance corporals. Privates rank the lowest in the British Army.

Although there are still marked distinctions in status and pay between commissioned officers, warrant officers and non-commissioned officers, these dividing lines were far more evident in previous centuries than they are today, reflecting as they did the traditional, class-based attitudes and conventions of society at large. Soldiers' wives (unless themselves also

Opposite:
Two young
army children
photographed
with their parents
in Kent in the
early years of the
twentieth century.
Details of their
soldier father's
uniform and
medals suggest
that he is a drum
major who saw
action on the
Gold Coast.

Sergeant Clarence Stillwell pictured in 1915 with his young sons. They were to serve in the Territorial Army during the 1930s, before being commissioned for service in the Second World War, when both were killed.

'Goodbye, Daddy': with the band playing in the background, four army children wish their father farewell at Aldershot station during the First World War. A corporal in the Royal Army Medical Corps, he is probably bound for the Western Front.

serving soldiers, as is now becoming increasingly common) and children have always had civilian status, yet the ranks held by their soldier spouses and fathers have tended to dictate their treatment by the army authorities, as well as by fellow army families. In the past, officers' higher social standing, often going hand in hand with their private incomes (or those of their wives), generally resulted in a certain amount of independence from the army for their families, and certainly in better accommodation; officers' children have historically been more likely to attend independent boarding schools, too.

Army pay has never been noted for its generosity, and the rank-and-file soldier's wage was so meagre during the eighteenth century that, after compulsory stoppages, it was barely enough to support him, let alone a family. In addition, the army authorities discouraged marriage, regarding wives and children as unwanted nuisances who at best would distract their men from the serious business of soldiering, and might even cause significant disruption.

Since 1685, soldiers and junior officers had been required to ask their commanding officer's permission to marry, requests that were not always granted, particularly if the prospective bride was disapproved of for some reason. So if a soldier did marry during the eighteenth century, it was frequently without the knowledge or sanction of his superiors. This meant that many army children of that period (not all of whose parents were married) tended to grow up 'off the strength', that is, independent of the practical support – however limited – that the army extended to those whom it had accepted and recognised as being 'on the strength'. For the army would then assume a measure of responsibility for these fortunate few, providing sustenance, for example: half the food and drink ration issued to their husbands for army wives, and half- or third-rations for army children, according to their age.

THE SOLDIER'S SAFE RETURN.

Life was usually hard enough for 'off-the-strength' families, but if soldier husbands (or partners) and fathers were ordered abroad on active service, or to a garrison in a distant part of the British Empire, their dependants' situation became critical – even catastrophic – for they were banned from going too.

'The Soldier's Safe Return': a lithograph dating from around 1830 depicts the joy of the wife and children of an officer of the Life Guards on his return from fighting 'for love and liberty' to a comfortable-looking home.

Edward Penny's painting of around 1765 portrays the Marquess of Granby giving money to a sick soldier with a wife and children to support. Many army families lived from hand to mouth during the eighteenth century.

9

As well as being bound together by ties of affection – often extremely strong – many army families depended on their soldier menfolk's pay for survival. And because that money was paid directly to the soldier, without him, and without it, destitution loomed unless a family was able to fend for itself. Without large, organised charitable bodies and a welfare state to provide some sort of supportive social safety net (these would not be established until the late nineteenth and twentieth centuries), the situation of most abandoned families was desperate, and many young army children consequently went to work or did whatever was necessary to try to keep hunger at bay and a roof over their heads.

In 1800, the army's commander in chief, Frederick, Duke of York, stipulated that six (and sometimes up to twelve) on-the-strength wives per company of one hundred men (or four women per sixty soldiers) would be allowed to accompany them when posted abroad, thereby making official a previously informal practice. Which of the women went was decided by the drawing of lots the day before embarkation, and while army children were discouraged from travelling, many nevertheless did. The families who remained in Britain might receive a payment judged sufficient to enable them to travel to their home town or village, where they might have relatives who, theoretically, could support them. But after that they were on their own, and, under the terms of the Poor Law, many ended up being dependent on parish-provided poor relief, with older children being apprenticed to a trade (the boys) or domestic service (the girls); after 1834, and the passing of the Poor Law Amendment Act, the dreaded destination was often the workhouse.

They may have been considered the lucky ones, but permission to accompany their soldiers overseas did not mean that on-the-strength families had it easy. Indeed, most suffered – some terribly, and some even fatally – on the ships that carried tem to the foreign destinations to which their menfolk had been ordered, or while trying to keep up with an army on the march. The harrowing

Off-the-strength army wives and children were abandoned when their soldiers' regiments were ordered abroad, as portrayed in an illustration (part of the composite print 'Tommy Atkins' Married – Past and Present) that appeared in The Graphic newspaper in 1884.

first-hand accounts of those who took part in the retreat to Corunna between 1808 and 1809 during the Peninsular War are unsparing in their descriptions of the army women and children dying by the wayside. Rifleman Benjamin Harris of the 95th Rifles, for example, tells in his memoirs of seeing a mother dragging her young son along the road:

> At last the little fellow had not even strength to cry, but, with mouth wide open, stumbled onwards, until both sank down to rise no more... This was not the only scene of the sort I witnessed amongst the women and children during that retreat. Poor creatures!

The threat that Napoleon and France posed to Britain following the French Revolution of 1789 was so significant that a string of defensive fortifications was constructed along England's southern coast to repel an expected invasion. In the event, there was no incursion, Britain instead taking the war against France abroad, notably to the Iberian peninsula, during the Napoleonic Wars of 1803–15. In order to combat France, the British Army was both greatly increased in size and reorganised, a consequence of this being the granting of some concessions to on-the-strength soldiers' families, including, in 1812, the official establishment of regimental schools for the 'children of the regiment'. In 1797, infantrymen had received a pay rise, from 8d to 1s a day, although

This print, which was published in an 1889 issue of *The Graphic* newspaper, depicts army wives and children aboard a troopship being issued with warm clothing free of charge. Many would otherwise have frozen as they sailed into cold climes.

'All through walking with a soldier': a postcard of 1912 reflects the then-widespread view that soldiers typically had many children (and not always within wedlock).

stoppages (deductions) remained in place. In addition, the concerted barrack-building programme that was implemented at this time resulted in on-the-strength army wives and children being allowed to share a barrack room with their soldier menfolk – and dozens of their comrades.

Vacancies on the regimental marriage roll remained few and far between, however, and it was not until 1867 that marriage regulations were significantly slackened, with officers and regimental sergeant majors then being permitted to marry, along with 60 per cent of sergeants and 7 per cent of soldiers of lower ranks. This relaxation of the rules followed two sobering conflicts of the previous decade, the Crimean War (1853–6) and the Indian Mutiny (1857), which had highlighted not only the unsatisfactory conditions to which soldiers and their families were subject, but also the need for an efficient army. Further reforms, implemented between 1868 and 1874 by Edward Cardwell, the Secretary of State for War, set the framework for army life that remains recognisable today. These included the introduction of a 'localisation' system whereby infantry regiments were split into two battalions, one of which was posted abroad, while the other remained at the regimental depot, which was fixed at a particular place. Wherever their regiments were stationed, soldiers and their families were increasingly well catered for through the establishment of military hospitals, married

Five army children dressed in their best clothes surround a display of household objects intended to evoke a homely atmosphere. Seated alongside them in an early twentieth-century photographer's studio are their mother and father, who holds the rank of sergeant.

Robert and Margaret Patterson pictured with their children in Canterbury, Kent, shortly before the First World War. While Robert had served in the 20th Hussars, his sons opted for the 4th Dragoon Guards and 17th Lancers; his daughters all married soldiers.

quarters, schools (these were reorganised by garrison in 1887) and other facilities. In addition, it was made a soldier's responsibility to maintain his family financially, thereby leaving fewer deliberately abandoned wives and children destitute and a burden on the public purse.

Reflecting the changing fortunes of Britain and its place in the world, as well as of society as a whole, the way that soldiers' offspring have experienced growing up as 'children of the regiment' has not remained static since the 1870s. But in the general matters of postings, accommodation, life 'within the wire', schooling and entertainment, as well as the legacy of an army childhood, there is nevertheless common ground.

The married quarters that were built in the early twentieth century for army families at Tidworth Barracks, Wiltshire, were nicknamed 'Merthyr Tydfils' because they resembled Welsh miners' terraced houses.

FOLLOWING THE DRUM

MOST ARMY FAMILIES have accompanied their soldier husbands and fathers wherever they have been posted – if the military authorities have permitted them to do so (and sometimes even without official sanction). Their modes of transport in following the drum (travelling with the army) have conformed to the norms of time and place, and, similarly, their destinations have reflected Britain's changing global status, role and responsibilities over the last three centuries, with regular and peacetime stations within England, Scotland, Wales and Ireland, or Northern Ireland, often alternating with more distant postings whose locations have been dictated by international conflicts or the need for an armed presence to promote or protect Britain's interests abroad.

Overseas postings have sometimes exposed army children to disease, danger and death. Cholera killed many of the army children who are buried in Malta's cemeteries, for instance, and many more were lucky to survive the bombardment by Axis planes that the island endured during the Second World War. Some army children living in the Far East suffered imprisonment at the hands of the Japanese during this conflict, while army children were murdered by sepoy rebels around ninety years earlier, during the Indian Mutiny, most notoriously at Cawnpore. Yet for each tragic young individual who found himself or herself in the wrong place at the wrong time because of a soldier father's occupation, there are hundreds more who have benefited from the broadening of their horizons through accompanied tours of duty (postings during which soldiers are joined by their families).

British soldiers have always had to go wherever their country has required them, whether within the British Isles (where garrisons are maintained during peacetime) or abroad. The places where army children have lived therefore

A Married Soldier on the March in India.

14

Rebels threw the bodies of massacred army wives and children, including fifty-five children of the 32nd (The Cornwall) Regiment of Foot, down a well at Cawnpore in 1857, during the Indian Mutiny. It subsequently became a memorial to the dead.

mirror the course and events of British history. In earlier centuries, some youngsters were compelled to accompany their fathers to war, as occurred, for example, during the American War of Independence (1775–83), the War of 1812 (1812–14) and the Napoleonic Wars (1803–15); the last 'accompanied campaign' was the Crimean War (1853–6). More usually, however, their destinations have been 'family stations' – typically large, permanent garrisons established to maintain British interests overseas. As a result, many army children have been born abroad, sometimes to mothers who were residents of the countries to which their soldier fathers were ordered.

The earliest of Britain's foreign garrisons was established in 1662 in Tangier, now in Morocco, on the North African coast, a territory gained from Portugal following the marriage of Catherine of Braganza to King Charles II. Army wives and children were present there until their evacuation by ship

With a father in the Royal Engineers, Doreen Routledge (far right) and her siblings spent the Second World War in Malta. They are pictured amid the ruins of their married quarter in Valletta the morning after the Luftwaffe had bombed it.

15

This detail from a postcard dating from the late nineteenth or early twentieth century shows some of the married quarters at Floriana, Malta. Having had a presence there since 1800, British forces (and their families) finally left Malta in 1979.

between 1683 and 1684. Minorca was gained during the eighteenth century, finally being handed back to Spain in 1802, while Gibraltar was officially ceded to Britain by Spain in 1713 (and remains a British overseas territory, although it ceased to host a British Army garrison in 1991). Malta was given to Britain by the Treaty of Paris in 1814, a strategically valuable territory that gained its independence in 1964. Cyprus came under British administration from 1878 and became independent in 1960, although, with the creation of sovereign base areas at Akrotiri and Dhekelia, British soldiers and their families have continued to be stationed on the island into the twenty-first century.

The British Army's arrival in Egypt was initiated in 1882 at the invitation of its ruler, and it remained there until 1936, some troops staying on to protect the Suez Canal until their final departure from the Suez Canal Zone in 1956. Army families lived in Palestine during the British Mandate between 1923 and 1948. They were stationed in South Africa, too, following the Second Boer War (1899–1902), and, in the aftermath of the Second World War, in Libya and in Kenya (where a state of emergency due to the Mau Mau rebellion prevailed from 1952–9), as well as elsewhere on the African continent.

Britain's possessions across the Atlantic once included colonies and territories in Canada and, prior to the American colonists' declaration of independence from Britain in 1776 (following which 553 army children sailed with the British Army from Boston), eastern North America. The British West Indies included Dominica, Grenada, St Lucia and St Vincent, as well as Bermuda and Jamaica (where army families were still stationed after the Second World War), among whose dependencies was numbered British Honduras, or Belize. These were among the many places in the Americas that required the protection of the British Army and were consequently home to army children.

During the nineteenth and twentieth centuries, many more army children lived in Asia: in India; Burma (now Myanmar), until its independence in 1948;

Hong Kong (up to 1997); Singapore (until 1971); and Malaya (now part of Malaysia), where a state of emergency was declared in 1948 that lasted until 1960. England had gained Bombay (now Mumbai) in 1662, while the first British regiment to serve in India (the 39th Foot) had arrived in 1754, but it was the Indian Mutiny of 1857 that resulted in Crown rule, the reorganisation of Britain's armed forces there, and India consequently becoming the most frequent destination for army families posted abroad until its independence in 1947.

Following the Second World War, the largest concentration of British troops – and their families – was in the area known as the British Army on the Rhine (BAOR); this was BAOR's second incarnation, the first having existed after the First World War, between 1919 and 1929. Both armies were initially occupation forces based overwhelmingly in western Germany, although the primary purpose of the second BAOR was later to provide the first line of defence against a possible invasion of western Europe by the Soviet Union and its Eastern Bloc allies. (During the Cold War, some army children experienced the thrill of travelling on a military train across the Iron Curtain, through the Russian Zone, or East Germany, bound for their homes in West Berlin.) In the immediate aftermath of the Second World War, British army families were living in Italy, Trieste and Austria (many travelling there on the Medloc – Mediterranean Line of Communication – Express, a troop train that ran across Europe from the Hook of Holland to Villach between 1945 and 1955), as well as in other locations where occupation forces were temporarily stationed. Since the establishment of the North Atlantic Treaty Organization (NATO) in 1949, army children have also lived in the vicinity of various NATO headquarters – near Brunssum, in the Netherlands, for example.

By 1980, the number of 'family stations' abroad had been significantly reduced, and they were now concentrated mainly in West Germany, Cyprus, Gibraltar and Hong Kong. By 2000, only Germany and Cyprus remained common overseas postings, and cost considerations make it likely that army children will increasingly 'follow the drum' within Britain, if at all, in future decades.

Certain politically sensitive postings have exposed British army children to danger, for example, when EOKA was terrorising those connected to the British forces in Cyprus during the late 1950s, and the IRA was doing the same in Northern Ireland from the late 1960s to 1998. Yet perhaps the

Maggie Sorrell was about two when she was photographed in 1937 with her mother and father – who was in the Royal Army Ordnance Corps – in front of their bungalow on the island of Manora (then in India, now in Pakistan).

Soldiers on a March, an etching by George Moutard Woodward dated 1811, depicts the 3rd (The East Kent) Regiment of Foot (The Buffs) 'following the drum'. It may be a caricature, but many army children once travelled in this way.

greatest danger to life and limb that they have experienced over the course of history is when *en route*.

Before the age of steam, army wives and children trailed along behind columns of soldiers on the march. As camp followers, their place was with the baggage train, and most trudged along on foot, the luckier ones hitching a ride on a cart, baggage wagon or the back of a pack animal, while the more privileged officers' families rode ahead in coaches or on horseback. These modes of overland travel were always arduous for women and children, and could sometimes even be fatal. During the retreat to Corunna during the winter of 1808–9, for instance, some army mothers, 'in the unconquerable energy of maternal love would toil on with one or two children on their backs; till on looking round, they perceived that the hapless objects of their affection were frozen to death', as Sergeant Anthony Hamilton, of the 43rd Light Infantry, sorrowfully related.

Campaigning abroad, or reaching a foreign station, once necessitated sailing there, typically on a transport or troopship, usually a former merchant vessel converted for the purpose. As ever with the army, rank prevailed, and while officers' wives and children would usually be allocated small cabins to share, other ranks' families would be accommodated in dark, cramped, filthy and smelly conditions below deck alongside army horses, livestock and general cargo. Numerous army children were born in these foul conditions – and died in them, too, some of disease, and some when their ship capsized or was wrecked. In 1816, for example, thirty-eight children were among the dead when the transport *Seahorse* was wrecked off the coast of Ireland.

The introduction of trains and steamships helped to make the transportation of army families quicker and more comfortable during the

Army wives and children are shown living in dingy, if relatively spacious, conditions aboard a troopship in a detail from the composite print 'Tommy Atkins' Married – Past and Present (published in The Graphic newspaper in 1884).

nineteenth century, as did the motorisation of many types of transport during the twentieth century. Indeed, the relative cheapness and speed of travel enabled by post-war trains, buses, cars, ships, ferries, hovercraft and, most thrillingly for youngsters, aeroplanes (often chartered), allowed army children who attended British boarding schools to join their parents during the school holidays as a matter of course, even when 'home' was an exotic station such as Hong Kong. And as travelling became less perilous, being on the move – be it on a long sea voyage or a short flight – became a far more enjoyable experience.

Based on a sketch made aboard HMS Himalaya, this print portrays a rather chaotic-looking dinnertime for army families sailing on a troopship. It was published in The Illustrated London News in 1873.

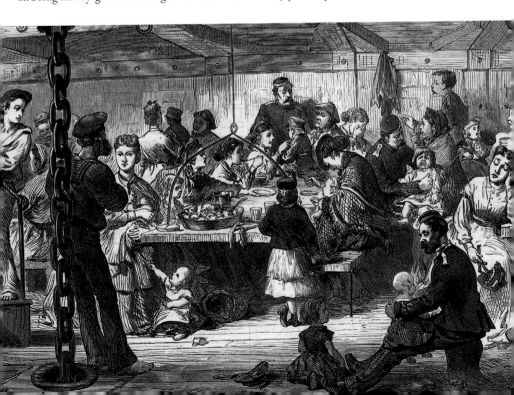

'PADS BRATS'

'ARMY BRATS' is one of the nicknames given to army children; others include 'barrack rats' and 'pads brats', both referring to buildings in which soldiers' families have historically been housed, that is, barracks and married quarters ('pads'). Over the centuries, army children have also been quartered in hirings: rented billets, lodgings, flats and houses, accommodation that has ranged in standard from the squalid to the relatively luxurious, depending on a soldier father's rank. Some have even lived under canvas – in army-issue tents – as well as in wooden hutments and Nissen huts.

Families who go wherever the army orders them can never be sure what standard of housing they will find on their arrival, or even whether their new home will have been left as clean as they would like (despite the typical 'marching-out' inspection of every army-supplied quarter conducted at the end of an accompanied tour of duty). In recent years, with foreign postings being fewer, army families have increasingly been able to settle themselves in Britain, and consequently also to buy and live in homes that, as their own properties, are not subject to army interference, or to its taste in decoration and furnishings.

It is difficult to imagine that bedding down on the floor in the corner of a noisy, pungent barrack room packed with soldiers could be an improvement on any alternative type of living arrangement, but this was indeed the case for most eighteenth-century army children. From 1792, at the same time as a barrack-building programme was implemented at coastal locations around Britain in response to the threat of a French invasion, on-the-strength army families were granted the privilege of a barrack-room billet. In return, wives and older daughters were expected to perform domestic tasks, such as washing and sewing, for officers and men, perhaps for a small sum. Off-the-strength families continued to be left out in the cold, however, being forced to fend for themselves wherever it was that following in their military menfolk's footsteps took them. For them, 'home' was usually some form of cheap rented accommodation, typically a shared space in a mean abode. From 1800, those soldiers who had married with their

Opposite:
A soldier from a Highland regiment paces outside his married quarters in Aldershot, Hampshire, holding his baby. His wife stands in the doorway, while his older children (one barefoot) sit nearby. This print first appeared in *The Graphic* in 1871.

Some married quarters at Hounslow Barracks, Middlesex (seen here at the end of the nineteenth century or the start of the twentieth), took the form of low-rise apartment blocks.

commanding officer's permission were sometimes allowed to leave their barracks in order to join their families in their lodgings at night, as were officers. Having more money made all the difference to officers' families, whose rank-appropriate accommodation tended to be the most comfortable that could be rented in the vicinity of the barracks, or wherever the army required their husbands and fathers to be.

Living in a cramped barrack room was a mixed blessing for on-the-strength families during the nineteenth century. Advantages included being together as a family and having a roof over their heads. But among the considerable disadvantages could be counted a lack of privacy (only a blanket draped across a corner to screen it off from the rest of the room separated the family from the other soldiers) and the children's constant exposure to pipe smoke, bad language, drunkenness and occasionally also violence and indecency. (The presence of teenage 'daughters of the regiment' among so many men was often singled out as a particular cause for concern.) Recalling the first night that he spent in a barrack room in 1843, Trooper Buck Adams described it as being

> … occupied by twenty-five single men, not reckoning the married men who had their wives and families. Each family occupied one corner of the room, which was hidden from the rest at night-time only by a sheet fastened across the corner. The scenes I witnessed and the language I heard…

A long table was usually positioned along the central length of the room, at which the meals cooked in the barrack room were eaten, with rows of iron beds set at close quarters on either side of it. No special provision was made for children, who usually curled up on the floor for the night, unless a soldier was away, leaving a vacant bed to creep into. Infectious diseases – including cholera and tuberculosis – were rife, spreading rapidly through barrack rooms that were cramped and unhygienic (and most contained communal urine tubs that sometimes doubled as wash basins). Yet not only were

Modern Married Quarters:
"Haw! Are You Crowded Heeaw?"

A distinguished visitor surprises an army family (and maybe two) living in 'modern married quarters', as depicted in *'Tommy Atkins' Married – Past and Present* (published in *The Graphic* in 1884). The bed and table indicate bedsit-type accommodation.

numerous army children conceived in these corner-system conditions, they were born into them, too.

There were also times when on-the-strength families found themselves living under canvas, similarly sharing with unmarried soldiers a tent in camp, or else a timber-framed hut within a more permanent encampment.

Although some army families permitted to live in barracks had been fortunate to be allocated a room to themselves (albeit often shared with other families) from the 1830s, only twenty of the 251 British barracks offered such separate accommodation by the 1850s. The situation was a little better in India, where most rank-and-file families initially inhabited small, cabin-like spaces off the barrack room, some later being assigned modest bungalows within the barrack yard.

A colourful view of the married quarters at Dagshai, which today lies within the Indian state of Himachal Pradesh. This hillside cantonment was occupied by the British for a century, from 1847 to 1947.

Dagshai. Married Quarters

Soldiers' Married
Quarters, Peshawar

Thick walls, large open windows and blinds to screen out the hot sun are a feature of these soldiers' married quarters in Peshawar, as photographed in around 1910. Then in India, Peshawar is now part of Pakistan.

The standard of army-provided accommodation improved greatly for army families with the introduction of married quarters following the Crimean War, largely prompted by concerns about the morality, poor health and high death rates of soldiers and their families. (Indeed, as Staff Surgeon Julius Jeffreys, writing in 1858, observed of the British Army in India, 'the mortality of the barrack children is appalling'.) So from 1860, whenever a new barracks was constructed, so, too, was separate housing for the wives and children of married soldiers, often in the form of blocks of one-room apartments or of 'hutments' within the barrack compound. Forty-two families were catered for at the barracks in Hounslow, Middlesex, in 1860, for instance, in rooms leading off long verandahs; effectively a bedsit, each room included a hearth (enabling cooking), a bed, a crib and two cupboards, with shared lavatories situated at the end of the verandahs. Married quarters were increasingly being provided for army families posted abroad, too, with the style of building often mirroring local conventions. Officers' married quarters within Indian military cantonments, for instance, were typically bungalows with verandahs to help combat the heat.

More barracks were built following Cardwell's reforms (1868–74) and the consequent creation of regimental depots, and, with them, more – and more modern – married quarters, whose size, fixtures and fittings varied according to the rank of the soldier *paterfamilias*. Describing these new and improved married quarters, 'Red Cross', writing in *The Navy and Army Illustrated* in 1896, commented:

> They are bright and airy, well ventilated, gas and water laid on. In almost every case a family, even without children, are given a two-room quarter, the number of rooms being increased in proportion to the number of children: thus, where there are five children, the regulation provides for four rooms and a scullery.

Rank, length of service and family size remained the determining factors in the allocation of quarters, with the better-quality, larger accommodation going to higher ranks, and only then to army families with many children.

Married quarters would never be luxurious, but they were a huge improvement on the corner system and all that had gone before. In providing

some privacy and self-sufficiency, they enabled army children to experience a more normal family life than previously, even if they were still living within the bounds of their father's barracks, depot or base.

When the numbers of army families arriving at foreign family stations made it financially worthwhile, groups of married quarters resembling civilian housing estates were constructed to accommodate them. This occurred particularly within the military cantonments in India in the century before independence, and in West Germany during the second half of the twentieth century, where many 'patches' (of married quarters) were built 'outside the wire'. Flats were provided as well as houses, especially in places

At the time that this photograph was taken (during the early decades of the twentieth century), the married quarters that made up 'C' lines at Bulford Camp, in Wiltshire, were huts, or hutments.

Married Quarters, Bulford Camp.

Despite lacking individuality, the red-brick terraces of married quarters that were constructed at Bulford Camp during the first half of the twentieth century were an improvement on the hutments shown above.

25

where land was at a premium, as in Hong Kong. Among the advantages for army families of living in such close-knit communities has always been mutual support (particularly when soldiers are away on exercise or on active service), and a ready, if constantly changing, supply of playmates for army children.

If a vacant quarter was not available, if a British Army presence had not yet been fully established at the foreign location to which families had been posted, or if British troops were not envisaged as being stationed there for long – in BAOR during the 1920s, or Trieste during the late 1940s and early 1950s, for example – the army tended to requisition or rent civilian accommodation ('hirings') from local landlords. In times of housing shortages (immediately after the Second World War, for instance), Nissen huts have occasionally served as married quarters, too, and army families have also been given temporary accommodation in hotels and hostels.

In places where living space was limited, married quarters tended to be flats, such as those shown in a postcard dating from the first half of the twentieth century of an apartment block on Kennedy Road, in Hong Kong's Mid-levels.

Whatever form their housing has taken, army families have typically paid rent to the army for (usually subsidised) quarters and army-issue furnishings, which, as army property, have customarily been inspected and checked against an inventory on marching out. The army has not, however, provided 'adornment' (ornaments and pictures, for example), as 'Red Cross' noted in 1896, observing that it was nevertheless 'simply astonishing how home-like and comfortable a soldier's wife manages to make her surroundings'. Indeed, when they are regularly on the move, it is precisely a family's personal possessions that help to make a house a home. Because their loved ones and personal possessions are the only constants

Corrugated metal covered the roof and walls of the married quarters that the Rutledge children lived in during the mid-1950s, after their father, who was in the Royal Engineers, was posted to Perham Down, near Tidworth, Wiltshire.

in their lives, most army children feel that 'home' is not defined geographically, but is instead where the heart – their family – is.

One of the consequences of the British Army's reduction in size since the end of the Cold War has been the selling-off of married quarters – also known as service family accommodation (SFA) – on the open market. As a result, children of civilian families are now living in houses once inhabited by generations of army children, who are in turn increasingly growing up in properties owned or rented by their parents, rather than the army. This is one aspect of army life that has thus become more civilianised.

The sender marked an 'X' on the front of this postcard, by an open window with a family gazing out, scrawling 'married quarters, R Signals, BAOR' on the back. The clues suggest a hiring in Germany in the 1920s.

27

LIFE 'WITHIN THE WIRE'

SINCE their general introduction during the later nineteenth century, many of the married quarters that have served as army children's homes have been situated 'within the wire', that is, inside the boundary that has typically separated a barracks, regimental depot or other form of military base from the civilian world surrounding it, for purposes of efficiency or security. Even when living 'outside the wire', army children have paid regular visits to these hubs of military activity, mainly because army-provided facilities and services that they have been entitled to use have often been located there, creating essentially self-contained communities.

Such amenities include sources of sustenance and provisions; hospitals and medical services; churches, which, as well as being places of private worship, are often also the focus of ceremonial occasions; collection points for mail sent via the British Forces Post Office (BFPO); and frequently also messes, libraries, sporting facilities, cinemas and other venues dedicated to providing entertainment. Crèches, kindergartens and schools – infant, primary and secondary – attended by army children have sometimes been located within the wire, too, especially abroad.

The establishment of regimental depots throughout Britain was a consequence of the implementation of the 'localisation' scheme following Cardwell's reforms of 1868 to 1874. Major garrison towns, such as Aldershot in Hampshire (established in 1854), already existed, but these

Many army children have lived in married quarters constructed within the confines of a barracks, such as those at Devizes Barracks (also known as Le Marchant Barracks), in Wiltshire, seen here in an early-twentieth-century postcard.

A postcard showing some of Catterick Camp's features (including a theatre and post office) long before 1973, when this North Yorkshire army base became Catterick Garrison. Even then, it was too large to be literally enclosed within 'a wire'.

large military bases were now supplemented by the development of camps and barracks such as that at Devizes, Wiltshire, where Le Marchant Barracks (which was constructed in 1878) served as the Wiltshire Regiment's headquarters until 1959.

In accordance with the 'localisation' system, while one of a regiment's battalions remained at its depot in Britain, another would be posted abroad – often, before 1947, to the Indian subcontinent. There, army families would generally live within cantonments (permanent military camps), moving up to the cooler, and more relaxed, hill stations – such as Simla (today Shimla), in the foothills of the Himalayas – when the heat became unbearable. A similar annual migratory pattern was followed elsewhere, too: in Jamaica, for example, where the Newcastle military cantonment (established in the Blue Mountains in 1841) was a far more salubrious location for children and adults alike than Up-Park Camp, which was situated in yellow-fever-prone Kingston; while in Cyprus, the Troodos hill station provided temporary relief from the less healthy conditions of the Limassol garrison. Although their overall purpose was the same, hill stations' facilities varied, with the tents of Troodos contrasting with the very British-looking permanent structures of Simla, for instance.

Whether the military base around which their lives revolved was a depot or a barracks, a cantonment or a camp, or a huge garrison or base like that constructed at Rheindahlen, in West Germany, between 1952 and 1954, there was usually little need for twentieth-century army families to venture 'outside the wire', for their most basic needs – accommodation, food, medical care – were all contained within it. Indeed, this was often considered crucial in those postings where the safety of British soldiers and their families might be at risk from a hostile populace or terrorist group.

The hilly situation of the military cantonment at Newcastle, Jamaica, is evident in this picture-postcard view of the Blue Mountains dating from the first half of the twentieth century. Its altitude made it a cooler and healthier spot than Kingston, the island's capital.

"Greetings from Jamaica"
Newcastle Military Cantonment.
19 Miles from Kingston.

A summertime view of Quetta Cantonment, c. 1910. Now in western central Pakistan, Quetta was once part of India. During the Raj, cantonments like this contained married quarters, churches, markets and other facilities.

Being supplied with food rations was a vital perquisite for on-the-strength soldiers' families during the nineteenth century, with army children receiving either a quarter or a third of a soldier's ration, according to their age. Although this entitlement was eventually phased out for families stationed in Britain, the regulations of 1867 specified that a ration allowance should still be paid to wives and children whose soldier menfolk had been ordered away for more than four days.

Army families overseas continued to receive actual food rations, however, with children being allocated a quarter of their father's share. A rationing system overseen by a unit's quartermaster was in operation in the British Army on the Rhine even as late as 1954, as set out in a guide of that date issued to army families:

Food for families is now available from three sources: The Army (RASC Rations), NAAFI, and German shops ... There are five main scales which provide a full ration. These are known as Scale 1 (Husbands and Boys over 14); Scale 2 (Wives and Children over 12); Scale 3 (Children 5–11 years); Scale 4 (Children 1–4 years); and Scale 5 (Infants 0–1 year) ... The meat issue is one of the most important items in the family ration.

Army children sometimes also ate home-grown food, as an article entitled *'Tommy Atkins' Married*, published in *The Navy and Army Illustrated* in 1896, explained: 'In most garrisons, both at home and abroad, each married soldier has a piece of ground in which he cultivates potatoes and other vegetables sufficient for his family'. Otherwise, when in Britain, army families shopped locally, at civilian shops, as they also did abroad (circumstances permitting), although generally mainly for fresh produce or exotic goods. After 1920, when the Navy, Army and Air Force Institutes (NAAFI) came into existence, most army families stationed overseas bought staple foodstuffs at reasonable rates from the supermarket-like shops established by the NAAFI within the wire, as well as British goods that would otherwise be unobtainable, including clothing and toys.

It was not until the second half of the nineteenth century that army children began benefiting from army-provided medical services. Before then, army wives – and their offspring – were on their own when it came to coping with matters of life and death, and with all manner of ailments in between. What medical attention there was was typically reserved for soldiers, although regimental medical officers were at least permitted to prescribe medication to on-the-strength families from 1824. Numerous army children whose parents could not afford private medical treatment were therefore born, and often died, by the wayside while on the march, at sea, or in the overcrowded barrack rooms that offered ideal conditions for contagious diseases and infections.

The poverty and ill-health of many of the army wives and children who had been separated from their soldier husbands and fathers during the Crimean War (1853–6) prompted such charitable bodies as the Central Association in Aid of the Wives and Families of Soldiers Ordered on Active Service to arrange emergency medical attendance for them. From 1892, the Soldiers and Sailors Families Association (SSFA) provided 'SSFA sisters' – state-registered nurses – from its district-nursing service to attend to army families posted abroad in their married quarters.

Following the Crimean War, the army itself began to assume greater responsibility for the health of its soldiers' families, albeit in a distinctly military manner, the 73rd Foot's standing orders of 1858 stating, for example: 'The women and children will attend the medical inspection once

The Cambridge Military Hospital was opened in Aldershot, Hampshire, in 1879. Army children later received treatment at the Louise Margaret Hospital that was constructed alongside it in 1897; this became the Louise Margaret Maternity Hospital in 1958.

a week, or oftener if required'. This measure was primarily concerned with controlling diseases that might threaten soldiers' health, but the army's medical services gradually expanded to cater more fully for illnesses and conditions specific to childhood (and females). As increasing numbers of military hospitals were built from the later decades of the nineteenth century, so wards were set aside especially for women and children (notably at the Louise Margaret Hospital, which was attached to the Cambridge Military Hospital in Aldershot from 1897 to 1995).

British military hospitals (BMHs) were similarly established abroad, and countless army children were born or treated at such hospitals in Gibraltar and Hong Kong, or at Rinteln, Iserlohn and Münster (and others) in West

When this postcard was printed, the British military hospital on Europa Road, Gibraltar, was still relatively new. It began treating forces' personnel and their families in 1904 and closed in 2008.

Germany and elsewhere; many also lived nearby if their parents worked at the hospitals. Indeed, twentieth-century army children received medical and dental treatment from doctors of the Royal Army Medical Corps (RAMC), dentists of the Royal Army Dental Corps (RADC), nurses of the Queen Alexandra's Military Families Nursing Service (QAMFNS) and later the Queen Alexandra's Royal Army Nursing Corps (QARANC), and from other health professionals, military and civilian.

Another of the stipulations of the 73rd Foot's 1858 standing orders reads:

> Women and children will attend regularly their respective places of worship every Sunday. An absence report will be sent in every Monday morning, signed by the Quartermaster.

In practice, 'respective places of worship' usually meant either a Church of England or a Roman Catholic church, and the Sunday service that most soldiers and their families attended was at the garrison church, which was often situated within the wire. Until 1946, this demonstration of communal worship was accompanied by the pomp and ceremony of the 'church parade', with the soldiers marching to church from their barracks, and their wives and children dressed in their Sunday best. Similar ceremonial church services were (and are still) held on significant regimental anniversaries, as well as on Remembrance Sunday.

Then, as now, services were led by army chaplains, or padres, who had been ordained as ministers, of various Christian denominations, before joining up; there were Jewish chaplains, too, from 1892. From 1796, the chaplains were also charged with recording the births, baptisms, marriages, deaths and burials of their flocks of army families when stationed abroad.

A church parade at Hargraves Barracks, Gibraltar, most likely photographed shortly before the First World War. A small group of smartly dressed children stands between the ranks of soldiers and the military drummers.

A twenty-first-century view of Troodos Cemetery, Cyprus, looking to the south-west. Numerous army children who died prematurely at the nearby hill station were buried at this peaceful location from the later decades of the nineteenth century until 1934.

It was these padres, too, who conducted army children's baptism and funeral ceremonies, and who were present at their burials, often in military cemeteries in Britain (at Tidworth, Wiltshire, for instance) and abroad.

Maintaining contact with friends and relations, in Britain and elsewhere, has always been vital for peripatetic army families. Before the advent of personal computers, the internet and mobile phones, the main way of staying in touch was by mailing letters through the British Forces Post Office – as the latest incarnation of the 200-year-old army post office is called – each station abroad being represented by a particular BFPO number. Rather than being delivered to their married quarters, however, incoming mail was usually held at a collection point within the wire. From birthday cards posted by grandparents, through letters from pen pals, to 'blueys' (aerogrammes) sent by soldier parents on active service, most non-electronic mail addressed to army children has historically arrived via an army unit in this way. Similarly, the BFPO has provided an emotional lifeline in delivering letters from their parents to army children at boarding schools.

An army child lets off steam (to the left) on the occasion of a parade held in India in 1933 to mark the birthday of the king, George V, who was also emperor of India.

SCHOOLING

T HE ARMY may have been slow to accept, accommodate and otherwise assume responsibility for soldiers' families' welfare, but there is one area in which it has been progressive in comparison with civilian society: that of army children's schooling. For despite difficulties caused by lack of funds and high levels of mobility, it has generally tried to provide its soldiers' youngest dependants with a good education, either through schools established in the United Kingdom to prevent soldiers' children from falling into destitution; through regimental, garrison and depot schools that educated children of the regiment wherever they went; through the service schools that taught army children worldwide following the Second World War; or through the financial allowances that have helped countless forces children to attend boarding schools.

Some schools have been excellent; others less so. Some army children have excelled academically; others have struggled or have felt disengaged. The same could be said about civilian schools – many of which army children have attended – and about any children. The crucial difference between the children of civilian parents and army children – who are, after all, themselves civilians – however, is the frequency with which soldiers and their families are required to move: every two years, on average, since the Second World War. The first day at a new school is always tough, and when a child has go through it time and time again, with new friends continually having to be made and different teachers and curricula adjusted to (especially following the demise of regimental and garrison schools), the consequences may be negative and harmful to army children's chances in later life. Indeed, a disrupted education is a price that many army parents have thought too high to pay for togetherness, which is why they have opted to send their children to boarding schools.

Two publicly funded boarding establishments were among the first to cater specifically for soldiers' sons and daughters. Both the Hibernian Asylum (later the Royal Hibernian Military School), which was founded in Phoenix Park, Dublin, Ireland, in 1769, and the Royal Military Asylum,

An etching depicting two children of the Royal Military Asylum, with their school in Chelsea visible in the background. They are dressed in the uniforms that boys and girls were required to wear at the asylum in 1813.

subsequently the Duke of York's Royal Military School, which was established in Chelsea, London, in 1801, were intended to educate the orphaned or abandoned children of soldiers. As the petition to King George III requesting the incorporation of the Royal Hibernian Military School explained, its purpose was to preserve them 'from Popery, Beggary and Idleness and to train them up so as to become usefull Industrious Protestant Subjects'. Most of the boys who attended these establishments either joined the army or were apprenticed to learn trades on leaving at the age of fourteen, the girls usually being destined for domestic service or factory work, and later marriage and motherhood.

Similar institutions followed in the paths of the Royal Hibernian Military School (which moved to Shorncliffe, Kent, in 1922, before closing in 1924) and the Royal Military Asylum. The Caledonian Asylum (later the Royal Caledonian Schools) began to educate the children of Scottish soldiers in London in 1819, relocating to Bushey, Hertfordshire, in 1902; 'the Caley' survives as the Royal Caledonian Schools Trust. The purpose of the Royal Soldiers' Daughters' Home (today the Royal School), which opened its doors to soldiers' daughters in Hampstead, London, in 1855, was to train them for a life in domestic service or as army schoolmistresses. Like the Duke of York's Royal Military School (situated, since 1909, in Dover, Kent), the Queen Victoria School in Dunblane, Scotland – another boarding school – still educates service children over a century after its founding in 1908.

Underpinning the establishment of most of the early 'asylums' for army children was the charitable desire to prevent the offspring of soldiers who had fought, and often died, for their country from being forced by circumstance into lives of poverty, crime or prostitution. The regimental schools that educated on-the-strength children during the nineteenth century were similarly concerned with ensuring that they would be equipped to live useful lives. This laudable aim was not entirely altruistic, however, for the sons of soldiers frequently followed in their fathers' footsteps in enlisting in the army, while daughters often married into the military. Investing in their schooling would therefore directly benefit the army in the long term, while in the short term, attending lessons kept boisterous children occupied for a while.

There had been a regimental school as early as 1675, at the Tangier garrison. It and its successors during the eighteenth and early nineteenth centuries (typically funded by the officers of the regiment) were primarily

The Royal Soldiers' Daughters' Home in Hampstead as it appeared in around 1910. It was founded in 1855 'to nurse, board, clothe and educate the female children, orphans or not, of soldiers in Her Majesty's Army killed in the Crimean War'.

intended to teach uneducated soldiers basic reading and reckoning skills. The schooling of soldiers' children was considered secondary. In 1812, however, the Duke of York charged commanding officers specifically with encouraging the education of soldiers' offspring. He stated:

> The aim is to give the Soldiers the Comfort of being assured, that the Education and Welfare of their Children are objects of their Sovereign's paternal Solicitude; and to raise from their Offspring a succession of Loyal Subjects, brave Soldiers, and good Christians.

The children and staff of the regimental school of the 1st Battalion of the Northamptonshire Regiment (formerly the 48th Foot), photographed in India during the 1890s. The teaching staff includes a schoolmaster, schoolmistress and *munshi* (Urdu teacher).

To help achieve these aims, the secretary of war, Lord Palmerston, provided public funds for the establishment, lighting and heating of a regimental schoolroom in every barracks, in which young soldiers and army children would attend lessons. As at the 'asylums', the boys might be taught trades, such as tailoring and shoemaking, while the girls would be instructed in sewing, knitting, laundering and other 'housewifely' or 'industrial' skills by suitably qualified army wives or older daughters. The children would also be schooled by regimental schoolmasters – or 'serjeant' (sergeant) schoolmasters – in the 'three Rs'. From 1840, civilian army schoolmistresses (renamed Queen's Army Schoolmistresses in 1927) were employed to teach the girls, and later also infants, so that most

An army schoolmaster sits at the centre of a group of women, some most likely army schoolmistresses (and probably also army wives and daughters). The group posed for this photograph at Deepcut Barracks, Surrey, in about 1910.

regimental schools, depending on their size, were staffed by at least one army schoolmaster and schoolmistress, as well as an assistant.

By 1867, around nineteen thousand army children were being educated in a range of subjects at the regimental schools (many in specially constructed, dual-purpose 'chapel–schools'). Twenty years later, the regimental schools were replaced by larger garrison schools. By then, their

The board held by the girl at the centre of this group of children, who are flanked by their teachers, states that the photograph was taken at the garrison school in Verdala, Malta, in May 1921.

'Army School, Portsmouth' says the sign that identifies this class of between-the-wars children in Hampshire as the sons and daughters of serving soldiers.

Children can be seen at the centre of this postcard (and soldiers to the left), in front of Buena Vista School, Gibraltar. To the right, the large building at the foot of the mountain is the British military hospital.

male teachers were members of the Corps of Army Schoolmasters (founded in 1845), which, in 1920, became the Army Education Corps, a 'Royal' prefix being added in 1946. The corps also ceased to be responsible for educating army children in 1946.

By 1920, there were nearly two hundred army schools, some in garrison towns in the United Kingdom, but most in garrisons overseas, where, with no civilian alternatives, there was the greatest need for them. Civilianisation came in 1946, when local education authorities were charged with running

army schools in the United Kingdom, and with sending civilian teachers on secondment to schools abroad. In the same year, the British Families Education Service (BFES)was established to educate army children in BAOR. In 1969, the Service Children's Education Authority assumed responsibility for the education of all service children: Royal Navy and Royal Air Force youngsters, as well as army children: this was supplemented by the Service Children's Schools (North West Europe) Defence Agency in 1991. In 1996, the Service Children's Education agency, funded by the Ministry of Defence, took over.

The infant, primary and secondary schools – some newly constructed, others established within requisitioned or rented buildings – that all of these administrative bodies managed at different times at family stations the world over remained essentially the same. The aim was to ensure that forces' children would be well equipped to take their places as adults in British society, which is why service schools mirrored their civilian counterparts in the United Kingdom in terms of their organisation and subjects taught, sports played, and examinations sat (including the Eleven Plus, O levels or GCSEs, A levels, and tests for other qualifications and certificates).

Army child Maggie Sorrell (the tallest girl at the back of the group) attended the Venice Children's School between 1946 and 1947. Maggie and her small group of fellow pupils were taught by soldiers at this temporary school in Italy.

Barbara Messenger is pictured second from right in the front row at her service primary school at Sennelager, West Germany, in 1958. Her father was then serving in the Royal Electrical and Mechanical Engineers (REME).

41

The queen's cypher and the words 'Service Schools' were printed on the front of the exercise books issued to army children who attended service schools during the 1970s.

Service Schools

A postcard displays scenes photographed during the 1950s at Prince Rupert School, a boarding school for service children established at a former German naval barracks in Wilhelmshaven, West Germany, in 1947. (The school has been located in Rinteln since 1972.)

Most service schools have been day schools, with pupils often being driven to them on green army buses; in potential trouble spots, armoured vehicles escorted some to school. Some army children were once even taught on the move – aboard the troopships transporting them from one posting to the next.

Because postings in certain countries were widely scattered after the Second World War, some Cold War-era service schools accepted boarders, including Prince Rupert School, King Alfred School, Windsor School and Kent School in (West) Germany, Slim School in Malaya, Bourne School in Malaya (later relocated to Singapore) and St John's School in Singapore. A far higher proportion of army children have historically been sent 'home' to Britain to board, however, usually at public schools. Until 1946, in accordance with prevailing social norms, it was officers' children who were most likely to attend boarding schools in Britain. Thereafter, financial assistance in the form of the

Boarding School Allowance (later the Continuity of Education Allowance), combined with an increasing recognition of the long-term consequences of an education disrupted by 'turbulence', meant that most army families at least considered the boarding-school option.

Attendance at boarding school may minimise disruption to schooling, then as now, but the separation of family members, and the physical and emotional distance inevitably created, can be a high price to pay. Indeed, in the days before air travel drastically reduced journey times, army children with parents stationed in India, for example, might not see them for years at a time. Homesickness, too, has blighted many an army child's years at boarding school. Yet boarding schools have always offered undeniable advantages, including continuity of education and keeping the same friends for longer than a few months or years.

When stationed in Britain, recent generations of army children have attended local civilian day schools. This educational option is not without its problems either, though, for while the frequency with which most army children have moved in their short lives has helped them to be adaptable, fitting in is not always easy when teachers and fellow students have little understanding of the army lifestyle. That said, many army children feel that the life experiences that they have gained through travelling with their families more than compensate for any educational disadvantages.

The sign outside Bourne School in Singapore, where the school reopened during the mid-1960s following its closure in Kuala Lumpur, Malaya (now Malaysia).

An aerial photograph showing the location of King Alfred School, whose premises had been constructed for the German navy on the Grosser Plöner See at Plön in Schleswig-Holstein. This service secondary school in West Germany educated boarders between 1948 and its closure in 1959.

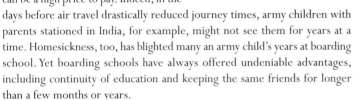

ENTERTAINMENT

CHILDREN always emulate what they see around them, weaving it into their games, so it would be surprising if army children had not played at being soldiers over the centuries, especially the boys. Maybe banging a toy drum served as preparation for enlisting in the army as a drummer boy (during the eighteenth century, the young sons of soldiers who had been killed in action while on accompanied service overseas often did just that). In any case, most army children have played with the same types of toys and games as their contemporaries in civilian society, perennially popular choices being dolls for girls and toy weapons for boys. Playmates of the same age and background were usually also plentiful for nineteenth- and twentieth-century children of the regiment, with streets, areas of common land and gardens within the wire and around married-quarter patches serving as their playgrounds (proper playgrounds were frequently provided, too).

Yet for most army children during the eighteenth and nineteenth centuries – except, perhaps, for some officers' children – playtime was limited by their families' lack of income, as well as by social norms. Many young army daughters once spent much of their free time helping their on-the-strength mothers wash and sew for the regiment, for example, while useful or educational pursuits would anyway have been encouraged over more frivolous games.

As the concept of leisure and various types of entertainment became more accepted and widespread during the twentieth century, however, so army children benefited from the sporting facilities, cinemas and clubs that were established within the wire. Radio and television services also began to play an increasingly important part in both entertaining service children stationed abroad and keeping them abreast of the cultural references familiar to their peers in British mainstream society. For these relatively well-travelled youngsters, one of the most priceless advantages of an army childhood has furthermore always been the opportunity to venture outside the wire in order to experience and explore the foreign countries that have temporarily provided them with a home from home.

Opposite:
The arrival of the Christmas pudding is the occasion of much excitement in this idealised illustration of a Christmas dinner for army children held aboard a troopship bound for the United Kingdom, which was published in *The Graphic* newspaper in 1889.

The soldier's children Miss and Master Tommy Atkins (the name is a traditional nickname for a British soldier) are depicted stereotypically, playing with toy soldiers and weapons, in these cards from a 'Funny Families' set dating from about 1910.

Keeping energetic children entertained during long sea voyages on troopships could not have been easy. One solution was tug-of-war contests, as depicted in this illustration from an 1887 edition of *The Graphic* newspaper, in which girls have been ranged against boys.

There was not much time or money available with which to indulge their children in centuries past, but most regiments tried to treat them to a Christmas lunch or party, and maybe, funds permitting, also to a present handed out by a soldier disguised as Santa Claus. As well as being held within the wire, often at sergeants' or officers' messes, Christmas lunches and children's tea parties were regularly given aboard troopships during the course of long sea crossings (it appears that the youngest passengers generally suffered far less from seasickness than their mothers). Another traditional regimental occasion still attended by many army children is the curry lunch, which dates back to the days of the Raj. Typically held on a Sunday, the gathering of army families at a mess to eat and unwind together is intended to reinforce the regimental spirit, or *esprit de corps*, and has also given countless army children a great opportunity to have fun together while the adults digest their curry.

Balls and teddy bears, toy guns and gliders, prams and dolls' houses, cranes and games – three children are clearly spoiled for choice when confronted by a NAAFI shop's toy display at Christmas in 1951.

The British YMCA club and canteen in Bielefeld, West Germany, shown in a postcard that dates from before 1957, when BFPO numbers replaced BAOR numbers. Many YMCA clubs permitted army children to use some of their facilities.

Army children, their mothers and ayahs (Indian nursemaids or carers) photographed in around 1910 listening to the military band playing in the cantonment gardens at Jubbulpore (now Jabalpur), in central India.

After the Second World War, as well as selling toys, games, sports equipment and other items of interest to children, the NAAFI operated clubs at military bases overseas. Although intended for soldiers' use, these clubs (which were organised by rank into facilities for officers, warrant officers, sergeants and junior ranks) usually either had family rooms or opened their doors to army families on occasion. Depending on their size, NAAFI clubs housed restaurants, bars, games rooms and lounges. Reading rooms stocked with British newspapers and magazines were another feature (and bookish army children also had access to reading material at libraries within the wire).

Some clubs had gift shops, too, and many army children were familiar with those similarly operated by the YMCA (Young Men's Christian Association) in many of the centres that the organisation established within military bases in West Germany. These sometimes had bookshops and canteens as well.

Most garrisons and military bases, in Britain and abroad, had a purpose-built theatre, or else a building within which plays and pantomimes, concerts and variety shows could be staged and films screened. Army children were sometimes in the audience, and sometimes among the performers – as choir members, for example. (Singing was on the curriculum in nineteenth-century army schools, as a report by 'Red Cross', writing in an 1896 issue of *The Navy and Army Illustrated*, explained: 'Music, both theory and practice, is taught and well taught, and a concert by soldiers' children is frequently a treat worth going some distance to enjoy'.)

After the Second World War, Combined Services Entertainment (CSE) was responsible for sending companies of actors and other entertainers to garrisons overseas to perform live variety shows. Previously part of the Entertainments National Service Association, the Army Kinema Corporation (AKC), like the CSE, was established in the aftermath of the Second World

British Forces Broadcasting Service broadcaster Bill Mitchell – better known as 'Uncle Bill' – held young Cold War-era listeners enthralled with his *Tales of Big Wood* radio programme. He is pictured here in his office at BFBS Cologne (Köln), West Germany.

49

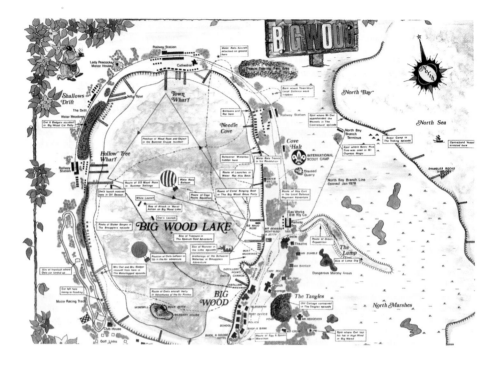

An intricate map shows details of the imaginary world of Big Wood created by the BFBS radio broadcaster Bill Mitchell ('Uncle Bill'). The animal characters in his *Tales of Big Wood* included Owl and Water Rat.

War to maintain cinemas on military bases for soldiers and their families stationed around the world. It was merged with its Royal Air Force counterpart in 1969 to form the Services Kinema Corporation, which in turn became the Services Sound and Vision Corporation (SSVC) in 1982. Many an army child has spent countless Saturdays at the cinemas run by these bodies, watching age-appropriate British and American films.

The Services Kinema Corporation was not the only organisation to be drawn under the SSVC umbrella: Combined Services Entertainment became a branch of the SSVC, too, as did the radio and television arms of the British Forces Broadcasting Service (BFBS). BFBS had started out after the Second World War in West Germany as the British Forces Network, initially as a radio station, to broadcast the news from Britain, local weather forecasts and various light-entertainment programmes, including some for children, to forces' families living in BAOR. Many of the programmes were the same as those broadcast in Britain, supplemented by features from local stations around the world focusing on the news, interests and views of army families posted nearby. *Family Favourites* was a popular radio request programme broadcast from 1945 until 1980, while many army children listened to *Kinder Klub* during the 1950s and were devoted to 'Uncle Bill' (Bill Mitchell) and his *Tales of Big Wood* during the 1960s.

Since 1975, there have been BFBS television broadcasts, too. Nowadays these are beamed into service families' quarters via satellite, and there are channels dedicated to forces' children when once there were only a few slots, such as that occupied by the request programme *Birthday Time*. Recent generations of army children posted abroad have therefore shared in the popular culture of their 'civvy street' contemporaries. In addition, although many have watched British and American television series and films whose dialogue has been dubbed into their host nation's native language, they have not had to rely solely on local foreign-language radio and television stations for their news, education and entertainment.

Sport has always been considered crucial by the army for keeping its soldiers fit and focused, which is why football, hockey, rugby and cricket pitches, tennis and squash courts, swimming pools and other sporting facilities have been features of most barracks, garrisons and military bases for the past century or so. Although intended mainly for soldiers' use, many have been made available to army children, too, often through membership of clubs run in their spare time by soldiers or their spouses. Riding (particularly for the children of cavalry regiments), sailing, skiing and gliding were just some of the alternative sports on offer for those posted to Germany, for instance. Similarly, clubs catering for all kinds of hobbies, activities and interests – and youth clubs, too – have been set up for army children on the initiative of enthusiastic adults.

Branches of some British or international youth organisations were also established at family stations abroad, partly to ensure that the children of soldiers did not miss out on the opportunities available to their peers in civilian society, and partly to channel their energies into pursuing constructive interests. Chief among these during the twentieth century were the Boy Scouts and Girl Guides, and their respective equivalents for younger boys and girls, the Cub Scouts and Brownie Guides.

It is said that travel broadens the mind, and one of the lasting benefits of an army childhood for those posted abroad has been the opportunity to see the world and to learn more about other cultures. Speaking during a parliamentary debate in 1955, Nigel Nicolson, MP for Bournemouth

A Rheindahlen District Scout's cloth badge displays the Northern Army Group (NORTHAG) insignia, a Frankish battleaxe. NORTHAG was based at Rheindahlen, (West) Germany, from 1954 to 1993.

Army children often follow a soldier parent into a military career. Pictured at the end of the Second World War as a cadet in the Junior Training Corps, this teenage bugler joined the army on leaving school.

East, referred to his recent visit to West Germany, where he had met some service children:

> The children have an astonishing maturity and elasticity. They learn things with remarkable facility: to them geography is not a matter of books, but of places they have actually visited ... To them the Mohne Dam is a place where one can sail on a Saturday afternoon, and Belsen is the name of a primary school.

Some army children viewed the 'foreign' element of postings overseas as tourists; others made firm friends outside the wire. Some – in India and Hong Kong, for instance – learned to speak their nursemaid's native language, if not fluently, at least well enough to communicate effectively. Many more army children whose soldier fathers met their foreign-born mothers while stationed abroad have been bilingual, having been brought up to speak their mother's tongue. Service schools, too, have generally encouraged contact with local communities, fostering friendship and understanding through such joint ventures as concerts or charity projects.

Many former army children have reported that the combination of the peripatetic army lifestyle and their exposure to foreign countries at a young age has given them an incurable travel bug. Some feel especially compelled to revisit the places where they lived as children, often in the hope that seeing them from an adult perspective will help to put disjointed memories of their turbulent army childhoods into context.

While attending the army school in Rome, Italy, in 1946, Maggie Sorrell (centre left, in the patterned swimsuit) and her fellow pupils enjoyed day trips to local sights or beaches.

THE LEGACY OF AN ARMY CHILDHOOD

> Next year we shall be living in a different country
> That brought its soldiers home for lack of money

wrote Philip Larkin in his poem 'Homage to a Government', published in 1974. The poem ends:

> Our children will not know it's a different country,
> All we can hope to leave them now is money.

As the British Army becomes increasingly lean and based in the United Kingdom, Larkin's words still seem pertinent decades later, despite the debatable notion of money being British children's only legacy. In any case, an army childhood bestows its own legacy on those who experienced it, one with both positive and negative aspects.

In later life, generations of former army children report having 'itchy feet', for example, the legacy of a turbulent childhood that makes it hard to settle in one place, but has instilled a love of travel in them. Others question the concept of 'home', or a home town, feeling that they belong nowhere, yet are also at home everywhere. Some, especially those with foreign-born mothers or those who spent a significant part of their childhood abroad, have a stronger emotional connection to another nation than they do to Britain. Many have gaps in their education, but may feel that this is compensated for by the exposure to different cultures and life experiences that their army childhood gave them. Some regret not having been able to retain childhood friends, but believe that spending their early years on the move has made them self-reliant, adaptable and able to get on with anyone.

The list could be added to, but, in summary, there is no question that this unusual upbringing leaves a lasting legacy, and one that will continue to be passed on to army children as long as the peripatetic military lifestyle endures.

Photographed
outside a married
quarters in
Hamburg, West
Germany, in 1967,
this army child
has borrowed her
father's headgear,
on which the Royal
Signals cap badge
is visible, and her
mother's boots,
for a dressing-up
game.

FURTHER INFORMATION

BOOKS

Allen, Charles. *Plain Tales from the Raj*. Abacus, 1975.

Gibson, Clare. 'Minors on the March', *Ancestors*, 73, September 2008.

Holmes, Richard. *Redcoat: the British Soldier in the Age of Horse and Musket*. Harper Collins Publishers, 2001.

Holmes, Richard. *Sahib: the British Soldier in India, 1750–1914*. Harper Collins Publishers, 2005.

May, Trevor. *Military Barracks*. Shire Publications Ltd, 2002.

Neuburg, Victor. *Gone for a Soldier: a History of Life in the British Ranks from 1642*. Cassell Publishers Ltd, 1989.

Trustram, Myna. *Women of the Regiment: Marriage and the Victorian Army*. Cambridge University Press, 1984.

Venning, Annabel. *Following the Drum: the Lives of Army Wives and Daughters Past and Present*. Headline Book Publishing, 2005.

Williams, Colonel N. T. St John. *Tommy Atkins' Children: the Story of the Education of the Army's Children, 1675–1970*. Her Majesty's Stationery Office, 1971.

Williams, Noel St John. *Judy O'Grady and the Colonel's Lady: the Army Wife and Camp Follower since 1660*. Brassey's Defence Publishers Ltd, 1988.

USEFUL WEBSITES

The Army Children Archive (TACA) chronicles British army children's history and includes more links to relevant websites: www.archhistory.co.uk

For information on the Royal Military Asylum, Chelsea (today the Duke of York's Royal Military School), and the Royal Hibernian Military School: www.achart.ca and www.rma-searcher.co.uk

The website of the National Army Museum communicates the history and heritage of the British Army: www.national-army-museum.ac.uk

The website of the multi-branch Imperial War Museum, the museum of conflicts and wartime life from the First World War to the present day: www.iwm.org.uk

The website of the Army Museums Ogilby Trust (AMOT), the definitive guide to the regimental and corps museums of the British Army throughout the United Kingdom: www.armymuseums.org.uk

INDEX